T0413431

Showdown RIVALRIES

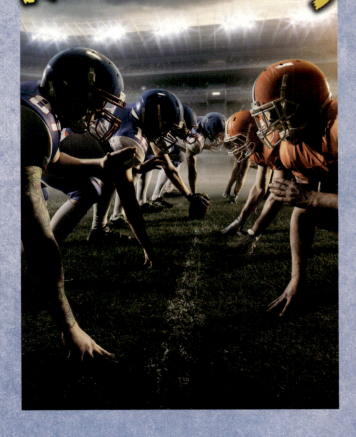

Kelli Plasket

Publishing Credits

Rachelle Cracchiolo, M.S.Ed., *Publisher*
Conni Medina, M.A.Ed., *Managing Editor*
Nika Fabienke, Ed.D., *Series Developer*
June Kikuchi, *Content Director*
Michelle Jovin, M.A., *Associate Editor*
Courtney Roberson, *Senior Graphic Designer*

TIME and the TIME logo are registered trademarks of TIME Inc. Used under license.

Image Credits: p.5 Philadelphia Daily News/MCT via Getty Images; pp.6–7, p.8, p.14 (right) Public Domain; p.13 (top) Trinity Mirror/Mirrorpix/Alamy; p.13 (bottom) Mark Wilson/Getty Images; p.14 (center) Romrodphoto/Shutterstock; p.15 (all) NASA; p.16 (top right) Peter Scholz/Shutterstock; p.17 National Archives and Records Administration; p.18 Francis Vachon/Alamy; p.19 The Advertising Archives/Alamy; p.20 Andy Lid/Getty Images; p.21 (top) Moviestore collection Ltd/Alamy; p.21 (bottom) Warner Bros./David James/Album/Newscom; p.22 Johnny Louis/JL/Sipa USA/Newscom; p.23 (left) CBW/Alamy; p.23 (right) CBW/Alamy; p.25 Jerry Wachter/Sports Illustrated/Getty Images; p.27 (top) Marka/Alamy; p.27 (bottom) Focus on Sport/Getty Images; p.28 Leonard Zhukovsky/Shutterstock; p.29 Jimmie48 Photography/Shutterstock; p.30 Zangl/Ullstein Bild via Getty Images; p.31 (top) SPL/Getty Images; p.33 (top) Popartic/iStock; p.34 (top) LittleNY/iStock; p.34 (bottom) George Vieira Silva/Shutterstock; pp.36–37 Andy Freeberg/Getty Images; p.38 John Mottern/AFP/Getty Images; p.41 WENN Ltd/Alamy; p.48 Dean Bertoncelj/Shutterstock; all other images from iStock and/or Shutterstock.

Library of Congress Cataloging-in-Publication Data

Names: Plasket, Kelli, author.
Title: Showdown : rivalries / Kelli Plasket.
Description: Huntington Beach, CA : Teacher Created Materials, [2019] | Includes index.
Identifiers: LCCN 2017055674 (print) | LCCN 2017059177 (ebook) | ISBN 9781425854911 (e-book) | ISBN 9781425850159 (pbk.)
Subjects: LCSH: Competition (Psychology)--Juvenile literature. | Competition--Juvenile literature.
Classification: LCC BF637.C47 (ebook) | LCC BF637.C47 P53 2019 (print) | DDC 302/.14--dc23
LC record available at https://lccn.loc.gov/2017055674

Teacher Created Materials

5301 Oceanus Drive
Huntington Beach, CA 92649-1030
www.tcmpub.com

ISBN 978-1-4258-5015-9
© 2019 Teacher Created Materials, Inc.
Printed in China
Nordica.072018.CA21800712

Table of Contents

Exploring Rivalries

For over 50 years, *MAD* magazine has featured a popular comic. *Spy vs. Spy* stars rival spies who look identical, except one is dressed in black and the other in white. In each comic strip, the spies try to sabotage each other. However, they often end up sabotaging their own goals as well. The **satirical** comic hints at a long-debated question about rivalries: Do they push people or groups to perform better, or do they hurt progress?

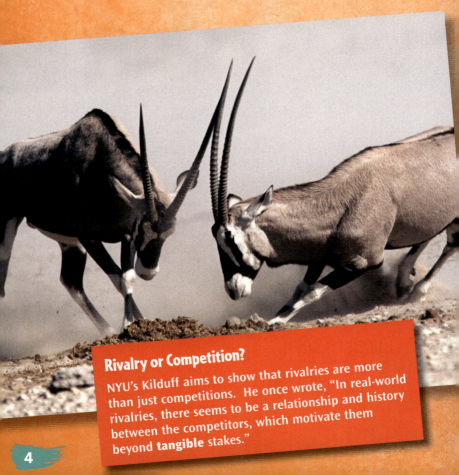

Rivalry or Competition?

NYU's Kilduff aims to show that rivalries are more than just competitions. He once wrote, "In real-world rivalries, there seems to be a relationship and history between the competitors, which motivate them beyond **tangible** stakes."

Gavin Kilduff, a professor at New York University (NYU), studies rivalries and competition. He says that rivalries often form when three conditions are met. First, the rivals are similar to each other. Their similarities increase the number of comparisons between them. Second, the rivals repeatedly compete against each other. Third, those competitions are evenly matched.

Let's look at some of the biggest rivalries in politics, business, sports, and culture from throughout history—starting with the Founding Fathers themselves.

Rival: A Word History

The English word "rival" comes from the Latin word *rivalis*. *Rivalis* means "one using the same stream as another." When people used to live as hunter-gatherers, they depended on natural resources. If two people lived in the same area, they competed for resources, thereby becoming rivals.

Spy vs. Spy

Great American Political Rivalries

Since the United States' founding, rivalries have been at the heart of shaping the young nation into a global superpower. It all started with the founders themselves.

Feuding Founding Fathers

The signatures on the Declaration of Independence may suggest the Founding Fathers were on the same page about how the country should be formed. They did agree on some things, such as American independence from Great Britain. But beyond that, the founders often fought and sometimes formed rivalries.

The Birth of Political Parties

Disagreements over how much power to give the federal government led to the birth of the two-party system. Hamilton and Adams were Federalists who wanted a strong central government. Jefferson led the Democratic-Republicans who wanted less federal and more state power.

Three of the fiercest rivalries were among members of President George Washington's own **cabinet**. They were Thomas Jefferson (Secretary of State); Alexander Hamilton (Secretary of the Treasury); and John Adams (Vice President).

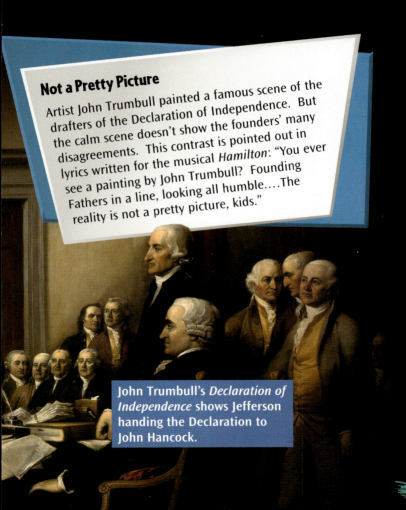

Not a Pretty Picture

Artist John Trumbull painted a famous scene of the drafters of the Declaration of Independence. But the calm scene doesn't show the founders' many disagreements. This contrast is pointed out in lyrics written for the musical *Hamilton*: "You ever see a painting by John Trumbull? Founding Fathers in a line, looking all humble….The reality is not a pretty picture, kids."

John Trumbull's *Declaration of Independence* shows Jefferson handing the Declaration to John Hancock.

George Washington (left) speaks with Hamilton (standing) and Jefferson (seated).

Forever Feuding

After Hamilton died, Jefferson placed a **bust** of Hamilton across from his own in the entrance hall of his home. However, Jefferson's bust was described as "colossal-sized," while Hamilton's was "life-sized." When guests noticed the busts, Jefferson would smile and say, "Opposed in death as in life."

Hamilton vs. Jefferson

Many historians say no event shaped the founding years of the United States as much as the personal and political rivalry between Jefferson and Hamilton. While serving on Washington's cabinet, the two men developed a deep rivalry over their differing viewpoints.

One crucial disagreement came over the establishment of a national bank. Hamilton fought for the bank's creation. Jefferson thought Hamilton wanted to form a **monarchy**. Hamilton thought Jefferson, a slaveowner, was a **hypocrite** for his talk of liberty. Their views later led to the two-party system.

Adams vs. Jefferson

Adams and Jefferson were friends. They had worked together to draft the Declaration of Independence in 1776. But their relationship fell apart over their opposing ideas on the best form of government.

In 1796, both Adams and Jefferson ran for president. Throughout the election, Jefferson claimed to not even know Adams was a candidate. Still, Adams won. Four years later, they both ran again, and this time Jefferson won. Adams skipped Jefferson's **inauguration**. They didn't speak for years after that.

Callendar's Concoctions

While running for president, Jefferson hired a man named James Callendar to spread rumors about Adams. The most damaging lie was that Adams wanted to go to war with France. Going to war was a deeply unpopular opinion in the years after the American Revolution. It was untrue, but voters believed Callendar and voted for Jefferson as president.

On January 1, 1812, Adams wrote to Jefferson to wish him a happy new year; Jefferson replied with a friendly letter back. The ex-presidents wrote each other to discuss history and politics until their deaths. They died on the same day: July 4, 1826. Adams' last words were "Thomas Jefferson still lives." Unknown to Adams, Jefferson had actually died hours before. Adams was right, however, that Jefferson's legacy would live on.

Adams vs. Hamilton

When Adams became president, he ignored Hamilton's advice. Hamilton used his influence with Adam's cabinet members to challenge Adams. In return, Adams fired the majority of the Hamilton supporters in his cabinet.

Just before the election of 1800, Hamilton wrote a 54-page pamphlet about President Adams. It criticized his public conduct and character. Though Adams lost, the letter did more damage to Hamilton. No longer seen as a party leader, Hamilton's political career was over.

THINK LINK

Unlike Adams or Jefferson, Hamilton never ran for president. Many people thought his opinions were too **divisive**.

> How might Hamilton's rivalries have contributed to his image of being too divisive?

> Should Hamilton have kept his feud with Adams, a fellow Federalist, a secret?

> What issues might arise from having a divisive president? Why?

Positions

- **Governor of Virginia**, 1779–1781
- **Secretary of State**, 1790–1793
- **Vice President**, 1797–1801
- **President**, 1801–1809

Political Party

Democratic-Republican

Thomas Jefferson
April 13, 1743–July 4, 1826

About Adams: "a blind, bald, crippled, toothless man."

Jefferson is responsible for bringing ice cream, macaroni and cheese, and french fries to the United States.

Position

- **Secretary of the Treasury**, 1789–1795

Political Party

Federalist

Alexander Hamilton
January 11, 1755–July 12, 1804

About Jefferson: "save us from the fangs of Jefferson."

Hamilton died in a duel in the same place where his son had died in a duel just three years earlier.

Positions

- **Vice President**, 1789–1797
- **President**, 1797–1801

Political Party

Federalist

John Adams
October 30, 1735–July 4, 1826

About Hamilton: "a brat…in a delirium of ambition."

Adams was the first president to live in the White House and was the father of President John Quincy Adams.

The Cold War

Personal rivalries such as the one between Jefferson and Hamilton can have long-lasting effects on politics. But national rivalries can be even more impactful—and damaging. One of the most famous national rivalries was the one that led to the Cold War between the United States and the Soviet Union.

After World War II, the two countries were among the most powerful in the world. But they had opposite **ideological** views. The Soviets wanted to expand their "sphere of influence" by spreading **communism** throughout Eastern Europe. The United States and its allies feared communism would threaten Western democracy.

In 1947, President Harry S. Truman signed the Truman Doctrine, which said the United States would fight the spread of communism. This act helped kick off the Cold War.

The rivalry spread into many parts of American and Soviet life. The two countries fought to be the best in everything from sports to science, attempting to show that their way of governing was the best.

"Hot" vs. "Cold" Wars

A *hot war* is a conflict that involves physical fighting using gunfire, bombs, and other weapons. In a *cold war*, both sides avoid direct military fighting.

bug disguised to look like a briefcase

Game of Spies

Spying was common on both sides during the Cold War. Spy gadgets developed during this time included an umbrella that fired poisoned darts (shown below) and listening devices, called *bugs*, placed in the heels of shoes.

Bul
Issued
In
the
w
C

The Space Race

The United States and the Soviet Union each wanted to be the leader of the Space Age. This rivalry was about more than just being the best in space; it was about military strength. Better space technology would lead to more powerful weapons.

October 4, 1957

The Soviet Union launches the world's first man-made satellite, *Sputnik 1*. The launch catches Americans off guard and kicks off the Space Race.

July 1958

The U.S. Congress passes the Space Act, which will create the National Aeronautics and Space Administration (NASA) from several government agencies.

April 12, 1961

Cosmonaut Yuri Gagarin (YOO-ree gah-GAHR-in) from the Soviet Union becomes the first human ever to visit space, shocking the world. A few weeks later, President John F. Kennedy announces plans to send an astronaut to the moon by 1970.

July 16, 1969

Apollo 11 blasts off with astronauts Neil Armstrong, Edwin "Buzz" Aldrin, and Michael Collins. Four days later, Armstrong becomes the first human to walk on the moon.

July 1975

American and Soviet space agencies join forces for the Apollo-Soyuz (SAW-yooz) Test Project. It helps open the door for future joint flights.

Many innovations that we use today came from money that was poured into technological advances during the Cold War. Global Positioning System (GPS) was created after the United States sought ways to track satellites, such as the Soviet *Sputnik*. The internet was developed in the 1970s to connect military research networks. Design innovations from the first moon boots, such as shock absorbers, are now used in athletic shoes.

Rulers During the Cold War

- **Beginning:** Premier Joseph Stalin
- **End:** President Mikhail Gorbachev

The Soviet Union stunned the world on November 3, 1957 when it launched the first living being into orbit—a dog named Laika (nicknamed Muttnick).

Gorbachev on the end of the Soviet Union: "We're now living in a new world. An end has been put to the Cold War and to the arms race….The threat of nuclear war has been removed."

Union of Soviet Socialist Republics (USSR)

Rulers During the Cold War

- **Beginning:** President Harry S. Truman
- **End:** President George H. W. Bush

The country's launch code for nuclear weapons from 1962 to 1977 was 00000000.

Bush's 1991 State of the Union address: "The end of the Cold War has been a victory for all humanity…and America's leadership was instrumental in making it possible."

United States of America (USA)

Not all advances were positive. During the Cold War, the United States and the Soviet Union began storing nuclear weapons. This led to the need for **disarmament**. The two nations agreed to the Test Ban Treaty of 1963. It banned nuclear explosions "in the atmosphere, outer space, and under water."

In the 1980s, President Ronald Reagan greatly increased military spending at a time when the Soviet economy was struggling. The Soviets couldn't keep up. By the time the Soviet Union dissolved in 1991, the Cold War was over.

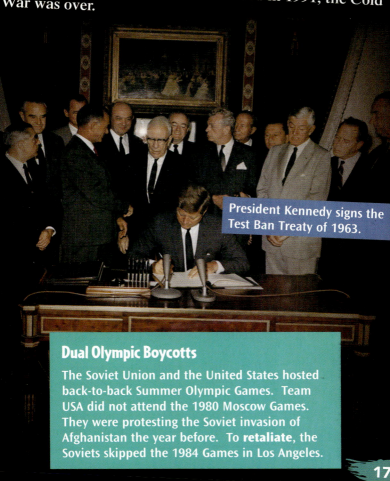

President Kennedy signs the Test Ban Treaty of 1963.

Dual Olympic Boycotts

The Soviet Union and the United States hosted back-to-back Summer Olympic Games. Team USA did not attend the 1980 Moscow Games. They were protesting the Soviet invasion of Afghanistan the year before. To **retaliate**, the Soviets skipped the 1984 Games in Los Angeles.

Pop Culture Face-Offs

The rivalries of the Cold War inspired many stories in popular culture. One of the most famous pop culture rivalries was *Spy vs. Spy*.

An Endless Rivalry

Cuban-born political cartoonist Antonio Prohías (ahn-TOH-nyoh pro-HEE-uhs) was the creator behind the satirical, wordless comic strip *Spy vs. Spy* for *MAD* magazine. Prohías began drawing the cartoon after fleeing communist Cuba for the United States. He had been accused of being a spy.

Spy vs. Spy was a hit, and it is still published today (now it is drawn by artist Peter Kuper). Its **longevity** is fitting for the title characters, who have spent decades pointlessly trying to one-up each other. "One isn't any better than the other—one is as **cunning** and tricky as his opponent," Prohías told a reporter in 1970. Both spies are evenly matched rivals. In that way, Prohías commented on the overall pointlessness of war.

Spy vs. Spy is now a popular game.

The First Spy

The first *Spy vs. Spy* was published in *MAD* in January 1961. It shows the spies at a café, trying to get the other to trip over spilled tea. The cartoon ends with the rivals being outsmarted by two thirsty cats.

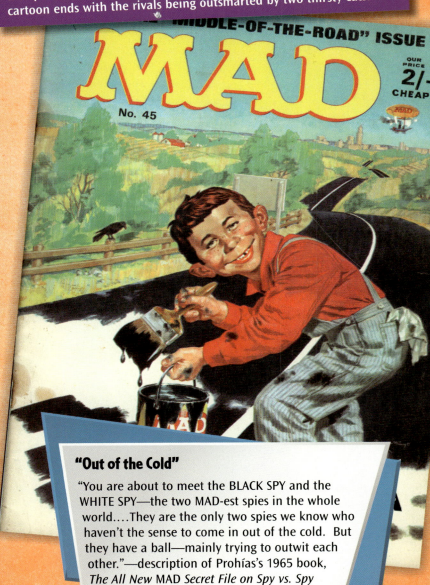

"MIDDLE-OF-THE-ROAD" ISSUE

MAD

No. 45

OUR PRICE
2/-
CHEAP

"Out of the Cold"

"You are about to meet the BLACK SPY and the WHITE SPY—the two MAD-est spies in the whole world....They are the only two spies we know who haven't the sense to come in out of the cold. But they have a ball—mainly trying to outwit each other."—description of Prohías's 1965 book, *The All New* MAD *Secret File on Spy vs. Spy*

Batman vs. Superman

Popular culture is packed with famous rivalries. Some are born in their stories, while some are imagined by fans. Both of those things are true with Superman and Batman.

Superman first appeared in comics in 1938, and one year later, Batman **debuted**. While they both want to maintain justice, the crime-fighters have opposing views on how to achieve it. Superman aims to inspire trust, while Batman operates on fear. In 1983's *Batman and the Outsiders No. 1*, a frustrated Batman quits the Justice League (an organization led by Superman) because he thinks it is too law-abiding. "We've always served as an example to the others," Superman says. Batman replies, "I never wanted men to *imitate* me—*only fear me*!"

When Superman and Batman fight in the comics, Batman often wins. But that doesn't stop rival fans from continuing the debate over who is the greatest superhero. On the sales charts, however, there is a clear winner— Batman comics regularly outsell Superman ones.

Superheroes Meet

In the 1952 comic *Superman No. 76*, Superman and Batman meet on a cruise ship. They quickly become friendly, competitive partners. The cover shows Superman yelling, "This is a job for Superman," and Batman replying, "No, this is a job for Batman!"

Alternate Names

Clark Kent (Earth name), Kal-El (Krypton name), Man of Steel, Last Son of Krypton

Backstory

An alien from the doomed planet Krypton, Kal-El was sent to Earth and raised by a couple on a farm. With superpowers that are charged by the sun, the Man of Steel is a symbol of hope.

Personality

friendly, loyal, **altruistic**

Strengths

super strength, super speed, X-ray vision, and flying

About Batman: "The most dangerous man on Earth."

Superman

Day Job
reporter

About Superman: "Deep down, Clark's essentially a good person…and deep down, I'm not."

Alternate Names

Bruce Wayne (birth name), The Dark Knight, Caped Crusader

Backstory

After a robber killed Bruce's parents in front of him, Bruce vowed to get revenge. He trained himself to physical perfection to become the Dark Knight—a crime-fighting nocturnal **vigilante**.

Personality

clever, cynical, **brooding**

Strengths

intelligence, extreme wealth, cool gadgets

Batman

Day Job
wealthy businessman

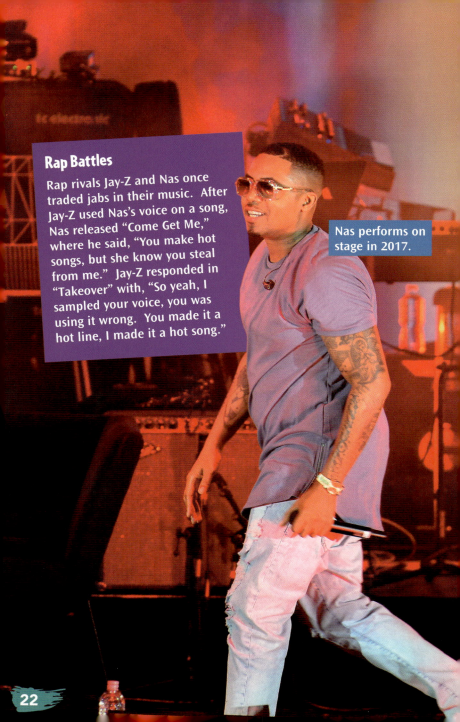

Rap Battles

Rap rivals Jay-Z and Nas once traded jabs in their music. After Jay-Z used Nas's voice on a song, Nas released "Come Get Me," where he said, "You make hot songs, but she know you steal from me." Jay-Z responded in "Takeover" with, "So yeah, I sampled your voice, you was using it wrong. You made it a hot line, I made it a hot song."

Nas performs on stage in 2017.

Music Battles

The celebrity side of popular culture is also packed with rivalries—especially among music fans. The Beatles and the Rolling Stones staggered the release of their singles and albums so they didn't compete on the charts. However, that doesn't stop their fans from debating which classic rock band is better.

The press can also fuel rivalries. In a 2014 interview, Taylor Swift hinted that her song "Bad Blood" was about fellow pop star Katy Perry for allegedly stealing Swift's back-up dancers. Perry responded on Twitter and later released a song about Swift. In 2017, Swift released her songs to free streaming sites on the same day Perry released her new album.

In no genre are rivalries more widespread than in hip-hop. Many rap artists will weave their **beefs** into their verses, as they try to outdo their rivals and prove themselves the best in the game.

Beatles vs. Stones

The Rolling Stones arrived on the music scene shortly after the Beatles. To stand apart, they remade their image as the "anti-Beatles." The Beatles wore matching suits and performed standing in place, so the Stones looked as messy as they could and started moving around on stage more.

23

Showdowns in Sports

Thanks to the competitive nature of the games, rivalries are everywhere in sports. Loyal sports fans spend lifetimes rooting not just for their home teams, but *against* hated rival teams as well.

Game Changers

The rivalry between basketball icons Larry Bird and Earvin "Magic" Johnson Jr. in the 1980s remains one of the most famous of all time. It's widely credited with saving a then-struggling National Basketball League (NBA).

Rising stars during their college basketball years, Bird and Johnson had their first high-profile matchup during the 1979 NCAA tournament finals. Johnson's Michigan State beat Bird's Indiana State in an exciting matchup. It is still the highest-rated college basketball game in history. After that, rival NBA teams recruited the players and they ended up on opposite coasts. Bird went to the Boston Celtics; Johnson went to the Los Angeles Lakers. Now, the rivalry stretched coast-to-coast.

Competitive Edge

NYU researcher Gavin Kilduff studied the rivalries and performances of 73 universities with NCAA **Division I** basketball teams. Kilduff found the teams performed better defense when competing against rivals and had more blocked shots. The results suggest that teams may try harder when playing against rivals.

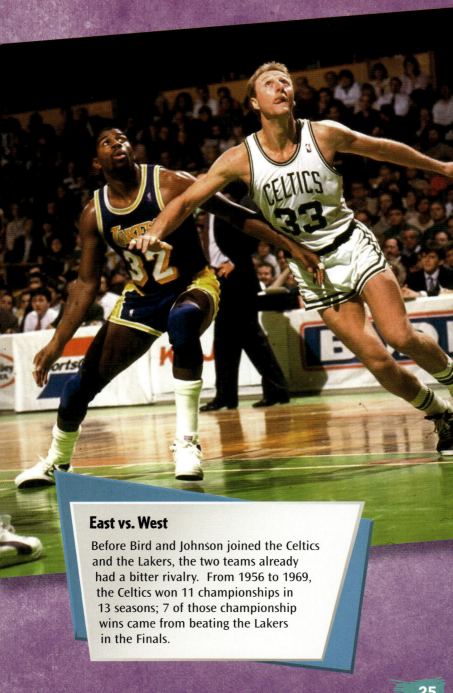

East vs. West

Before Bird and Johnson joined the Celtics and the Lakers, the two teams already had a bitter rivalry. From 1956 to 1969, the Celtics won 11 championships in 13 seasons; 7 of those championship wins came from beating the Lakers in the Finals.

Johnson and Bird became instant household names and dominated the sport for most of the decade. Even though they were both at the top of their games, the rivalry between them only grew in intensity. The rivals followed each other's game stats closely. During breakfast each morning, Johnson would check the newspaper for Bird's points and **assist count** before charting the numbers. "When those assists started going up, I knew he was doing what I was doing… making everyone better," Johnson said.

With Bird and Johnson leading the teams, the Celtics and the Lakers went head-to-head in three Championship finals—1984, 1985, and 1987. The Celtics took the first win, but the Lakers won the latter two.

The rivals disliked each other, until they talked over lunch at Bird's Indiana home while filming a commercial together. In 1992, they co-captained the gold-winning U.S. Olympic basketball team. After they retired from basketball, they remained friends. They even wrote a book together about their rivalry called *When the Game Was Ours*. In 2012, a hit Broadway play called *Magic/Bird* staged their feud.

The Dream Team

The 1992 U.S. Olympic basketball team was also known as the Dream Team. The nickname was half because the team won all its games in the Olympics by an average of 44 points. The other half came from the fact that it was the first time NBA players could play in the Olympics. Players such as Charles Barkley, Michael Jordan, Karl Malone, and Scottie Pippen stunned the world with their skills.

About Magic: "The first thing I would do every morning was look at the box scores to see what Magic did. I didn't care about anything else."

 Hometown

French Lick, Indiana

NBA Championships

1981, 1984, 1986

NBA MVP Titles

1984, 1985, 1986
(Finals: 1984, 1986)

NBA All-Stars

12

Larry Bird

Boston Celtics
Position: Forward

About Bird: "When the new schedule would come out each year, I'd grab it and circle the Boston games. To me, it was The Two and the other 80."

 Hometown

Lansing, Michigan

NBA Championships

1980, 1982, 1985,
1987, 1988

NBA MVP Titles

1987, 1989, 1990
(Finals: 1980, 1982, 1987)

NBA All-Stars

12

Earvin "Magic" Johnson Jr.

Los Angeles Lakers
Position: Point Guard

Tennis Titans

Tennis stars Serena Williams and Maria Sharapova have achieved what few in tennis do—a **career grand slam**. However, when they face each other, there's a clear winner—Williams has beaten Sharapova in 19 of 21 matches.

Their rivalry started at the 2004 Wimbledon Final, when a teenage Sharapova beat defending-champion Williams in an upset. Since then, Williams has beat Sharapova more times than she has any other top-10 player. "When I play [Sharapova], I know automatically I have to step up my game," Williams said. "I think that makes me play better."

About Sharapova: "I think my game matches up well against her. I love playing her. I think it's fun. I love her intensity....I just have the time of my life."

Serena Williams

Hometown
Saginaw, Michigan

Age Turned Pro | 14

Career Grand Slam Titles | 23

Career Winning Percentage | 85.5%

Sharapova has five grand slam titles, but if it weren't for Williams, she would have at least three more. Sharapova says she will keep working toward beating her rival again. "It's motivating because she's at a different level. She makes you go back to the drawing board," she said.

Making Money

While Williams dominates Sharapova on the court, Sharapova has her own title. She was *Forbes*'s Highest-Paid Female Athlete for 11 straight years. In 2016, Williams finally beat Sharapova on *Forbes*'s list. To unseat her, Williams had to earn a massive $27 million in one year.

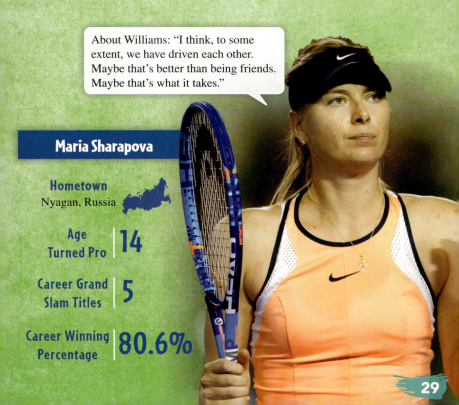

About Williams: "I think, to some extent, we have driven each other. Maybe that's better than being friends. Maybe that's what it takes."

Maria Sharapova

Hometown
Nyagan, Russia

Age Turned Pro | 14

Career Grand Slam Titles | 5

Career Winning Percentage | 80.6%

Business Battles

In the business world, rivalries can be fierce. With billions of dollars on the line, ignoring a rival can have costly consequences to **market share**. Company leaders will go to great lengths to top their rivals.

Coke vs. Pepsi

The Coca-Cola Company®, founded in 1892, controlled the soda industry for years. To stay on top, it relied on suing the competition. The Coca-Cola Company often sued soda makers with similar names, such as "Candy-Kola" and "Coke-Ola." In 1916 alone, Coca-Cola sued 153 copycats. By keeping other companies down, Coca-Cola stayed dominant.

The Pepsi-Cola Company® had a soda with a flavor that was similar to Coke, but with a product that was all its own. In 1934, Pepsi-Cola shocked Coca-Cola by breaking into the market when it began to sell 12-ounce bottles. These sodas cost five cents, which was the same price as Coke's 6-ounce bottle. After that, the rivalry was on.

Space Soda

In 1985, NASA agreed to let Coca-Cola send a modified can of Coke to space. Pepsi-Cola wanted in on the mission too, so it rushed to develop its own can. The astronauts tried both cans from space, but neither won the taste test—the soda was too warm.

Coke Goes to the Troops

During World War II, the amount of sugar people could buy was limited in the United States. Coca-Cola got around the limitations by selling soda to the military. American soldiers stationed around the world wrote letters home about the delicious, familiar taste of Coke. The move helped launch Coca-Cola into an international brand.

As time went on, Pepsi-Cola became more eager to beat Coca-Cola, but it struggled in southern states. So, in the 1960s, Pepsi-Cola launched the Pepsi Generation campaign. It was an effort to make Pepsi seem like a lifestyle choice.

Then, in the 1970s, Pepsi-Cola began conducting blind taste tests, in which people wore blindfolds and tasted drinks. They found that people slightly preferred the sweeter taste of Pepsi to Coke. So, in 1977, Pepsi-Cola launched the Pepsi Challenge ad campaign. This move angered Coca-Cola.

By 1984, Coke's once strong market lead over Pepsi was almost gone, and Pepsi had begun outselling Coke in supermarkets. The rivalry caused Coca-Cola to make one of the business world's most famous blunders. It launched the sweeter New Coke and dropped the old formula. Coke fans felt betrayed. Sales plunged, and Pepsi's market share overtook Coke's for the first time.

Coca-Cola quickly apologized to its customers and brought back its original formula, calling it Coke Classic. The reversal reignited love for the brand, and since then, Coca-Cola has kept a strong market lead over Pepsi-Cola.

Soda Out, Water In

Today, the soda industry as a whole is struggling as people seek healthier, less sugary beverages to satisfy their thirst. In 2016, bottled water passed carbonated soft drinks as the United States' largest beverage category by volume.

Source: 2016 U.S. Securities and Exchange Commission filings, and Interbrand

	Coke	Pepsi
Year Founded	1886	1898
Brand Value Worth	$73.1 billion	$20.3 billion
Ad Spending Per Year	$4.0 billion	$2.5 billion
Number of Employees	100,300	264,000
First Slogan	"Drink Coca-Cola."	"Twice as much for a nickel."

Nike

Year Founded	1964
Name Origin	Greek goddess of speed, strength, and victory
Best-Selling Shoe	Air Jordan III by Michael Jordan
Parent Company Market Share	34.7% (Nike)

Reebok

Year Founded	1958
Name Origin	Afrikaans word for a type of antelope
Best-Selling Shoe	Reebok Question by Allen Iverson
Parent Company Market Share	11.3% (Adidas)

Nike vs. Reebok

Nike® exploded to the top of the U.S. athletic shoe market in the late 1970s. But in the mid-1980s, rival Reebok® briefly took the top spot. Nike had mocked Reebok when it first introduced its Freestyle shoe. The Freestyle was a sneaker designed for the aerobic exercise craze of the time. But the Freestyle swept the women's market and sent Reebok's global sales skyrocketing from $300,000 in 1980 to $1.4 billion in 1987.

Nike rose back to the top after it convinced rookie basketball player Michael Jordan to sign on as a spokesperson for Nike. Nike gave Jordan his own shoe, called Air Jordans, which went on sale in 1985. Sales of Air Jordans hit $70 million within two months. In 1992, Reebok sponsored the U.S. Olympic basketball team's ceremony uniform. However, several members of the men's basketball team, including Michael Jordan, were sponsored by Nike. When the Dream Team won gold, the players covered the Reebok logo during the medal ceremony. After that, Reebok struggled until Adidas® bought Reebok in 2015.

Feuding Brothers

Shoemakers Adidas and Puma® were born out of a sibling rivalry. German brothers Adolf (called Adi) and Rudolf (called Rudi) Dassler had started a shoe company in their mom's laundry room. But a deep personal **rift** led them to split into two companies: Adi formed Adidas, while Rudi built Ruda (later changed to Puma). The brothers never spoke again.

Steve Jobs vs. Bill Gates

Steve Jobs and Bill Gates were born just seven months apart in 1955. They co-founded their respective technology companies, Apple® and Microsoft®, in the mid-1970s. Both saw promise in the **emerging** personal computer (PC) industry, but they had very different visions for what the future should look like.

Jobs, a smooth salesman with a passion for design, believed the desktop computer would improve users' lives at home, while Gates, a computer nerd at heart, saw desktop computers as a tool to help businesses be more efficient. Jobs was seen as a perfectionist when creating products; Gates was seen as willing to sell a passable product and improve it later.

Jobs vs. Dell

After Dell® founder Michael Dell said Steve Jobs should shut down his struggling company and give money back to shareholders, Jobs took offense and set out to beat Dell. Apple finally passed Dell in market value in July 2006. Jobs sent a company-wide email: "It turned out that Michael Dell wasn't perfect at predicting the future."

Early on, the two men worked together. Microsoft even wrote the **software** for Jobs' hit Apple II computer. The Apple II was the first mass-market computer to have icons, windows, and a mouse. Jobs thought his **hardware** with Gates's software would be a computer for everyone.

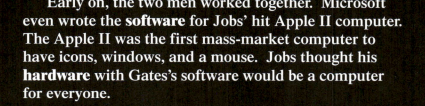

Words of Respect

Despite their different approaches to the business, Gates and Jobs clearly respected each other. When asked in a rare joint interview what they learned from each other, Gates admired Jobs's "**intuitive** taste, both for people and products." Jobs admired Gates's ability "to partner with people really well."

Steve Jobs (left) and Bill Gates (right) at a press conference in 1985

In 1983, Gates revealed Microsoft was developing Windows®, which would also feature icons, windows, and a mouse. A fuming Jobs accused Gates of stealing from Apple. Gates pointed out they both got the idea from Xerox®.

By the mid-1990s, Microsoft dominated the personal computer market with its software-only approach. That meant Microsoft did not make computers. Instead, it only sold Windows operating system to other computer makers. Apple focused on making both the hardware and software for a better user experience. That approach made Macs more expensive. Still, Macs developed a small but loyal fan base.

In 1997, Apple was nearing **bankruptcy**. Jobs announced at a Macworld convention that Apple had accepted an investment from Microsoft. Gates appeared by satellite, and the audience booed.

Over the next 15 years, Jobs used his second chance to change the industry with Apple's post-PC products, such as the iPod®, iPhone®, and iPad®. Meanwhile, Microsoft struggled to make a mark with similar products.

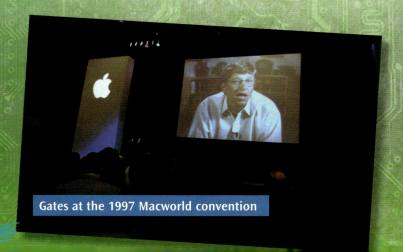

Gates at the 1997 Macworld convention

STOP! THINK...

Microsoft dominates the global market share for desktop operating systems. But mobile operating systems are a different story.

➤ How do you think Microsoft's software-only approach helped it reach nearly 90 percent market share?

➤ While iOS beats Windows on mobile platforms, Android tops them both. How do you think that happened?

➤ What conclusions can you draw from these charts about the future of Apple and Microsoft?

Desktop Computer Operating System Market Share (2017)

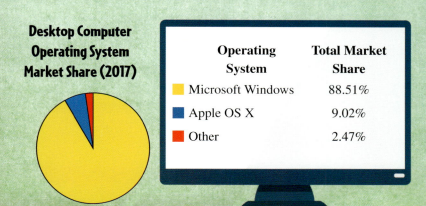

Operating System	Total Market Share
Microsoft Windows	88.51%
Apple OS X	9.02%
Other	2.47%

Operating System	Total Market Share
Google Android	64.36%
Apple iOS	32.72%
Other	2.61%
Windows Phone	0.31%

Mobile/Tablet Operating System Market Share (2017)

Source: NetMarketShare

Power of Rivalries

People love rivalries. That can be seen by the recent rise of rivalries in popular culture in recent years. The rivalry-driven musical *Hamilton* cost just over $12 million to make, but just one year after its release, it was making over $600,000 a week.

On TV, FX's *Feud* debuted in 2017. The first season showed the rivalry between Hollywood icons Bette Davis and Joan Crawford. The first episode of *Feud* quickly became FX's most-watched show of the year.

In his research, NYU's Kilduff has shown rivalry can motivate people to work harder. Rivalries often lead to higher performance on effort-based tasks. But Kilduff has also shown that rivalries can lead to a "win-at-all-costs" approach. Rivalries can certainly help people and companies grow, but finding the right balance is critical.

Rival, North Dakota

The town of Rival was formed in 1907 to compete with the nearby town of Lignite along a booming railroad. Though a post office was open for two years, the town never took off. Currently, only an abandoned grain elevator remains standing.

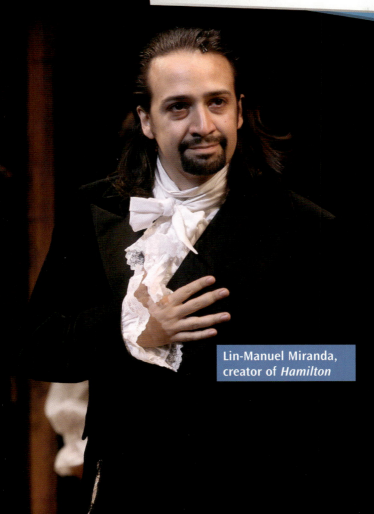

A New Basketball Rivalry

In the NBA, the Cleveland Cavaliers and the Golden State Warriors are playing their own version of the Lakers-Celtics 1980s rivalry. As of 2017, the two teams have faced off three years in a row in the NBA Finals. Golden State has come out on top twice.

Lin-Manuel Miranda, creator of *Hamilton*

Glossary

altruistic—unselfishly helping others

assist count—the number of times a player does something to help a teammate score

bankruptcy—a situation in which a company does not have enough money to pay its debts

beefs—fights or arguments between people or groups

brooding—very serious, gloomy

bust—a sculpture of a person's head, neck, and usually shoulders and chest

cabinet—a small group of people who give advice to the leader of a government

career grand slam—winning all major events of a sport

communism—a type of government in which the government, not the people, owns things

cosmonaut—an astronaut who works or worked for the space program of Russia or the former Soviet Union

cunning—clever and skilled, especially at tricking other people in order to get something

debuted—appeared before the general public for the first time

disarmament—process of decreasing the amount of weapons controlled by a military

Division I—the highest level of athletics a college can reach in the National Collegiate Athletic Association (NCAA)

divisive—causing many disagreements between people and causing them to form different groups

emerging—newly created or noticed and growing in popularity or strength

hardware—the physical devices used in or with computers, such as monitors, CPUs, and speakers

hypocrite—someone who claims to have certain beliefs about what is right but who acts in a way that goes against those beliefs

ideological—based on the ideas or beliefs of a group

inauguration—an official ceremony in which a person is newly elected to an office

intuitive—quickly or easily understood or learned

longevity—the length of time that a thing or person lasts or continues

market share—the percentage a company has in total sales for a particular category

monarchy—a type of government in which a king or queen rules over the people

retaliate—to do something bad to someone in an act of revenge

rift—a situation in which two people no longer have a friendly relationship

satirical—a form of humor that shows the weaknesses or bad qualities of a person, government, or society

software—the programs that run on computers and perform certain functions, such as games and word processors

tangible—able to be given a value

vigilante—someone who is not a police officer but who still catches and punishes criminals

Index

Check It Out!

Books

Bird, Larry, Earvin Magic Johnson, and Jackie MacMullan. 2009. *When the Game Was Ours.* New York: Houghton Mifflin Harcourt.

Donovan, Tristan. 2014. *Fizz: How Soda Shook Up the World.* Chicago: Chicago Review Press.

Isaacson, Walter. 2015. *Steve Jobs.* New York: Simon & Schuster, Inc.

Wertheim, L. Jon, and Sam Sommers. 2016. *This is Your Brain on Sports: The Science of Underdogs, The Value of Rivalry, and What We Can Learn from the T-Shirt Cannon.* New York: Crown Archetype.

Videos

Snyder, Zack, dir. 2016. *Batman v Superman: Dawn of Justice.* Warner Bros. Pictures. DVD.

National Geographic. *"Space Race."* video.nationalgeographic.com/video/space-race-sci.

Websites

AdWeek. *Apple's 'Get a Mac,' the Complete Campaign.* http://adweek.it/2k6qEqv.

Vulture. *What We Talk About When We Talk About Batman and Superman.* www.vulture.com/2016/03/batman-v-superman-c-v-r.html.

Try It!

Apple's "Get a Mac" campaign, starring Justin Long as "Mac" and John Hodgeman as "PC," ran for more than three years. A total of 66 different TV commercials aired during the campaign, all showing ways Apple felt its computers were better than Microsoft's PCs. Adweek called it the best advertising campaign of the 2000s.

Imagine you work for an advertising agency. The agency gives you a new client and tells you to make a video ad campaign.

- Pick a product category you're interested in researching—anything from cereals to apps.

- Research the market. Make a list of the companies making products in that category. Will you pick the market leader or an emerging product?

- Pick your product. Seek out any existing ads for that product, if available.

- Make a list of reasons that product is the best. What makes your product better than its rivals?

- Think about the audience for your ad. Who do you want to consider your product? What will get their attention?

- Decide which features you want to highlight in your ad. How will you convince viewers to buy your product? Will you compare it to rivals?

- Write a script and create storyboards for your ad.

- If possible, record your ad and share it with friends.

About the Author

Kelli Plasket was born and raised in southern New Jersey. She grew up rooting for the Philadelphia Eagles to beat their rivals, the Dallas Cowboys, and voting for *NSYNC to top the Backstreet Boys on MTV's *Total Request Live*. She graduated from the College of New Jersey with a journalism degree. Her first writing job was as a reporter for *TIME FOR KIDS* in New York City, covering everything from movies to politics. She now lives in New Hampshire with her husband and her cat, Mindy.

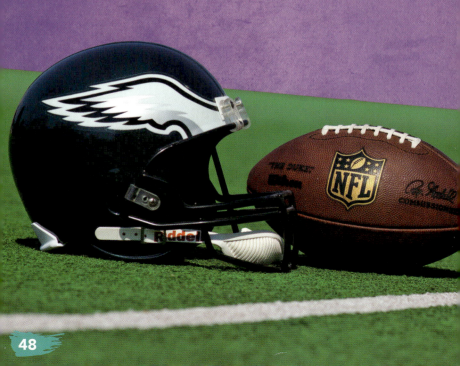